# ALL THEIR OWN

# ALL THEIR OWN

People and the Places They Build

by Jan Wampler

## Schenkman Publishing Company

Halsted Press Division

### John Wiley and Sons

New York—London—Sidney—Toronto

Copyright © 1977
Schenkman Publishing Company
3 Mount Auburn Place
Cambridge, Mass. 02138

Distributed solely by Halsted Press, A Division of John Wiley &
Sons, Inc. New York,

Library of Congress Cataloging in Publication Data
Wampler, Jan.
    All their own.

    1. House construction.     I. Title.
TH4812.W35          690'.8          76-25823
ISBN 0-470-15152-8

_Printed in the United States of America_

# DEDICATION

To the people in this book and to Marie, Kaaren and Amanda who shared this experience.

# FOREWORD

This is the way worlds begin. We want to shape matter because we want to live and life is where one can nourish the soul as well as the body. To nourish the soul by using the hands. Lifting stones, digging earth, putting sticks together. To combine things, to give them a place, make them carry loads, make them surround and let them enhance our vulnerable existence. The world begins only where it depends on our action.

The people that Jan Wampler discovered on his long trek through the continent hold a mirror to society and each of us is seeing something different from one's specific point of view. My own preoccupation with ordinary people's role in the life and death of built environments makes me see first of all a tremendous source of energy. The creative source of energy that throughout history made buildings and cities exist.

This book shows people first and buildings last. To admire their invention and praise their originality would only argue the poverty of our modern times existence. To point out that these people are outsiders who do their own thing regardless of society's norms would be misleading because they represent a typical dream: The old-fashioned American way to relate to the land and its other inhabitants. Those who build always want to relate. That is why building is a vital activity.

What makes this book important is that it makes us suspect that there is perhaps no other way left for ordinary people to relate through the act of building. Building is no longer a way for common people to take part in society's adventure. It has become the exclusive domain of professionals. Those who theorize and have expertise. The professionals who could dream for a generation or two that the world was there for them to shape and then to offer to ordinary people. To answer their needs and make them happy. The naive and dangerous attitude of a paternalistic elite that has forgotten that a civilization cannot be organized into existence because it must be cultivated through the day-to-day pains and experiences of everyday people.

To call these individuals exceptional—which of course they are—would be too easy. It would suggest that there is no use for them in the "real" world. Whereas it is exactly this source of unsophisticated creation that we should be concerned with as professionals. In our ignorance we have not even considered the possibility of its importance. And because of this neglect we are proposing more and more artificial environments. And make them. But that energy is there, and frustrated and polluted it finds its way elsewhere. People will finally destroy what they cannot build.

Let us not try to neutralize the book's message by inventing names for this kind of architecture. Let us not even call it architecture. Nor try to weave theories around it to protect ourselves. Because we know that our work will not hold if it does not recognize this force.

Nicolaas John Habraken

# INTRODUCTION

There was a time in this country when the building of your own home was common. The leaving of your mark or imprint on the land for your children and grandchildren—by making a farm, building a house or planting a tree—was the natural thing to do. Making do with what you had at hand was the general rule rather than the exception. The act of expressing one's life through building was common. People often left their mark on their building. It might be as simple as carving initials, a date, a message or a name over the fireplace, but it was there, an imprint of the builder.

Even later when building your own home was not so common, numerous books helped people choose homes that fit their needs. Page after page showed how to build or have a home built that would reflect the people who would live there. A home was thought of as something permanent, to change, to grow, to care for over the years and to be passed on to the next generation. It became a familiar place.

The apple tree planted in the yard with love and hope by one generation would bear apples for the next, and be pruned by the third generation. The fields of the farm would slowly become fertile; stone walls, fences, and out buildings would be added later. The home became the place to return to from a day's work or a year's journey. A place of your own.

The feeling we have towards our home today is entirely different. For most, the house has become one more commodity to buy, use and discard. The desire of a person to have an imprint on his or her home is difficult if not impossible to fulfill. In a country where families move to a new location every several years, and in an economy based on increasing consumption, it is difficult to think of permanence in housing which would allow for this personalization of a home.

The choices that most have in making a home are relatively limited. For the wealthy there is the option of hiring an architect. The house often turns out to be designed more for the architect than for the client. The client, for many architects, becomes an obstacle that must be conquered in order for the architect to express his or her creativity.

For those who cannot afford an architect, a second choice is housing that has been designed by architects but not for any particular person. For large housing projects, both public and private, the

architect relates to the board of directors or the administrator of the organization. The administrators or owners rarely live in the project they are administering, and the architect would generally consider the place unlivable from his or her point of view.

Another choice is housing designed by the builder or developer. These designs are usually based on economy and are not related to the people who will live in the houses. Potential buyers are normally offered a variety of options. The fact that the neighbor down the street is likely to select the same options reveals this choice as an empty gesture of individuality. By appealing to but not fulfilling our basic desire to express ourselves as different from one another, these superficial options do little but help developers sell houses.

The choices that a person has, then, are limited. If a person owns or rents a house, changes or alterations that might fit the person's needs are restricted since the time of stay may be short, and resale value of the house might actually be decreased by any change. The restrictions are many, and usually nothing can be changed without the owner's written permission. In some cases even a picture cannot be placed on the wall unless the owner is notified. Even the choice of furnishings has often been taken from us by being included in the package. Complete with furniture, lights, paintings and plastic flowers. The house has become another product for consumption with little or no identification with people living there.

Because of this and many other components of the American society, we have lost our relationship with the places in which we live. With this loss has come the loss of confidence to do, to build and to think for ourselves. We are constantly told that we must rely on professionals. Consequently, we have through the years relied on others to solve our problems, and now find it difficult to do the simplest task—let alone do something that expresses our own identity or affects our surroundings.

The way in which people affect their surroundings by dreaming, designing, changing or building a home has always interested me, as an expression of responsive architecture. Along with others, I have tried to develop an architecture not based on current styles, forms or monuments, but based on the desires of people. How to do it, how to start, how to encourage, is not always clear.

It was with this belief that I traveled through this country to see what people have built and to hear what people had to say about making and building. It would have been easier to refer to other

cultures and other times for examples of responsive architecture. But the examples are not always relevant as the customs and conditions are different. My search was one of traveling, stopping, seeing and listening. But in spite of my hit or miss techniques, I found many examples—more than I had expected—of people putting their imprint on their surroundings. They range from the most insignificant to the places shown in this book. The love of building I found in this country is best described in the following story.

While stopped at an intersection, I saw colors dancing in the trees beyond the assortment of interesting buildings. I stopped and walked past the buildings until I came to a house with a tower growing out of the roof. On the tower near the top was a window made of stained glass in the form of a spider web. It was this I had seen from the intersection. A woman glanced at me while tending her garden as if she had known me for a long time. She asked if I thought "the plants were too close together." She told me why the window was there.

For years she and her husband had dreamed of building a home—a place of their own. They eventually purchased a piece of land and worked many nights the first year, dreaming and designing their home. By the summer they were ready to build their home from left over material from his construction business. As they marked out the area for the home, they discovered an old shed was located exactly where they wanted to build and would have to be removed before construction could begin. In the shed was an open window where a spider had made a home. The sunlight transformed the web into a multitude of dancing colors. They talked and thought about destroying the spider's beautiful home in order to build their own home, and decided they would wait until the spider had left. While waiting they made a window from prismatic-shaped pieces of clear and stained glass like the spider's web. The next year they proceeded to build their home, building first the tower that held the spider's window.

I found many people that have expressed this love through the building of a home or the imprinting of places. It may be as simple as footprints of children and pets in the wet concrete or the embellishing of mailboxes along the road—each a different imprint of the people living there. Memories of the past woven into the design for a fence, a gate or a doorway. The special care and love given to the making of a window, filled with physical objects dear to the person. Whatever the form, there are people crying out to express themselves.

There are people who know who they are, what they want and what they can do for themselves. They are young, and old. They are building without the help of money, without the help of architects and without the burden of the norms of our society. Instead, they are taking care of themselves. They are thinking for themselves. And in most cases building with what is at hand.

They have shown that people are capable of building a home for themselves that transcends merely functional needs. It has become a home sensitive to their feelings—a statement of their lives. These men and women would be opposed to the idea that their places could suit anyone but themselves. Yet, they believe that many other people are capable of expressing themselves through their homes.

The places shown here should not be thought of as folk architecture or folk art, but simply as an expression of people. Their need to say that someone is here.

What may be gleaned from this book is a clue that these people have given us. The tremendous love, energy and originality that exists within all of us to affect our own lives within the physical world. These people have done so. It is my hope that all builders— architects, contractors, engineers, suppliers, public officials and technicians and we who use places, working together, can build a world—a responsive architecture—that can be all our own.

# DAVID BROWN
Boswell, British Columbia

To get there from the west we took highway number 3 across Canada—a small road winding around the mountains and lakes that ends at Lake Kootenay. A car boat was waiting there. We drove on and spent an hour crossing the lake and meeting the people we had seen on the road. Days afterward we saw their cars on the road and stopped and greeted them like old friends and exchanged stories. All because they didn't build a bridge.

On the other side of the lake is a home built of bottles. David Brown started work on the home in 1952 after retiring from the funeral business, and continued for the last seventeen years of his life. To many it was a strange home because Mr. Brown had built the home of bottles he had collected as a mortician. Funeral homes are always discarding the empty embalming fluid bottles and Mr. Brown thought he could use them to build a home. He traveled through Western Canada collecting 500,000 bottles from friends in the funeral business. He then began to build a home in a cloverleaf pattern with main rooms circular in shape. After building the home he continued to build lookout towers, bridges and walls down the hill towards the lake. Now his son continues building in the tradition his father started.

"Dad was just building a home, that's all he was trying to do, not make an attraction. Just meant to be our home. But then so many people started to stop. He loved people. People wanted to know what he was doing, he got a kick out of people laughing at him."

"This is something that just has grown, we want something done nice, we don't care how long it takes to get it done. We are building more to please ourselves. But if someone takes a picture of part of it then we know we have accomplished something because someone enjoys that part of it. That's how we get our praise. We watch that part of it, they put their kids beside to take a picture. You know then that you have done something nice."

The walls of the home, towers and bridges and other forms are made from bottles that are eight inches long and three inches square. They are laid in mortar like brick but since they are not porous it takes much longer to lay. The tops are left on the bottles to provide better insulation.

"Dad put so much into it, and the whole family, it's been a labor of love. Every year we have different ideas to add on more."

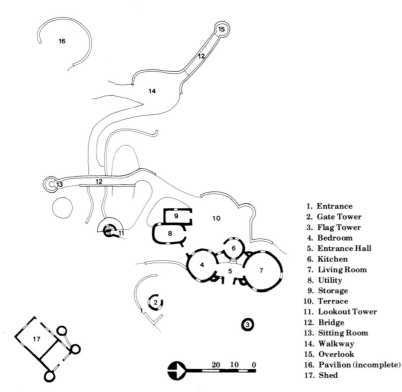

1. Entrance
2. Gate Tower
3. Flag Tower
4. Bedroom
5. Entrance Hall
6. Kitchen
7. Living Room
8. Utility
9. Storage
10. Terrace
11. Lookout Tower
12. Bridge
13. Sitting Room
14. Walkway
15. Overlook
16. Pavilion (incomplete)
17. Shed

20  10  0

"He had blueprints but you can't tell a person what you want as doing it yourself, eventually the blueprints went in the garbage. Like so many things you know it yourself."

# BOYCE LUTHER GULLEY
Phoenix, Arizona

Boyce Luther Gulley was born in 1883. He lived in Seattle operating a shoe store until 1927. Then he moved to Arizona for his health, leaving his wife and daughter in Seattle. There he worked on fulfilling a promise to his daughter to build a castle. He continued work on the castle until he died of cancer in 1945. He built about a room a year until it had eighteen rooms on several levels. The materials he used were what he could find: stone from the nearby mountains, wood from railroad cars, overbaked glazed tiles, refrigerator trays and automobile parts. His wife and daughter had not seen the castle until after he died. Now his daughter, Mary Lou Gulley, lives in the home he built for her.

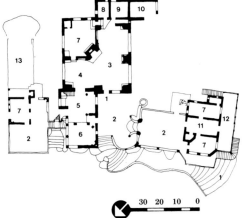

1. Entrance
2. Terrace
3. Living Room
4. Dining Room
5. Kitchen
6. Breakfast Room
7. Bedroom
8. Bathroom
9. Dressing Room
10. Storage
11. Hall
12. Porch
13. Pool (incomplete)

The first room he built was an L-shaped living room with wood from a boxcar and a large fireplace. The next year he added a bedroom up the hill from the living room and the year after the kitchen down the hill.

Windows were made from glass refrigerator trays that give a soft light in the rooms.

The mortar was mixed with water and a secret formula using goat's milk.

"You know, not only do houses look alike, but people are beginning to look alike."

# ELISE QUIGLEY
Eureka Springs, Arkansas

Lise Quigley wanted a new home. A home that was close to nature and large enough for her growing family. She knew her husband would not build a new one as long as the old one stood. So one June morning in 1942 when her husband went off to farm Lise and her children tore down their old house. At the end of the day when her husband came home the house was gone and she had moved into the chicken coop. She designed the new house in her mind but since she couldn't explain it to anyone she built a model of her idea out of cardboard and matchsticks. From that she and the family built the home with wood from the farm and with rocks she had been collecting since she was nine. For three years she built the two-story walls from her rock collection. In the walls are rocks from all over the country, petrified wood, fossils, an Indian grist stone and toy marbles that belonged to her sons. She wanted a home that would make you feel as close to nature as possible. To do this she made two foundations, an inner and outer, four feet apart. Between the two she planted tropical trees and plants that reach up the two stories. Like living in the woods.

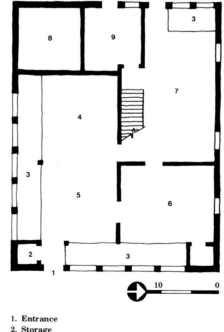

1. Entrance
2. Storage
3. Interior Garden
4. Dining Room
5. Sitting Room
6. Living Room
7. Kitchen
8. Water Tank
9. Bathroom

"I never thought of anybody else being interested in my house. But people started coming here to see it. I don't know why they didn't think of it themselves, but this has stimulated other rock hounds to build, so I've helped people too. I wouldn't want to do it again, but I'm glad I did it once."

"I covered the whole two-story building with my rock collection of the Ozarks, I've collected since I was nine. Everything on it is something pretty or odd."

"We really live off what God put in the world. You can practically live off a cow. She'll raise your meat, and if she's a real good cow, she'll raise an

extra calf for taxes. You can get
all the milk and butter and
cottage cheese you can use."

After the home was built she built gardens with birdbaths, birdhouses and arches all built with rocks she collected. Her husband collected bottles from which she made trees and placed on top of rock walls.

# EVERETT KNOWLTON
Stonington, Maine

As you come over a small hill on the road to Stonington you see the village ahead on the next hill. At first you're sure it's not real. Then the scale of houses makes you realize what it is—a miniature village. Everett Knowlton, born in Stonington in 1901, has worked for the State Department of Highways, in a stone quarry, and in a sardine factory. For over twenty years, in his spare time he has worked building his village. He started with one house and it just grew, complete with a church, store and schoolhouse. At first no one paid any attention to what he was doing; now he says four thousand people a year stop and talk and look at his village.

"Well, they're nothing to brag on, you know, most of them are all finished inside. Finished and furnished."

"I had to put one out there on the rock and ledges. I stuck one on there and it looked pretty good and I kept adding to it, that's all I know. Now I've got more than I can take care of."

The houses all have electric lights and are complete with furniture.

"I don't know one thing from the other about them. All I do is just build them. That's all. They come out the way they will. I never know what it's going to look like when I start it. I don't know nothing about that stuff. I just try not to get no two alike."

# BALDASARE FORESTIERE
Fresno, California

Baldasare Forestiere was born in Messina, Sicily, in 1879. He came to this country in 1902 when he was twenty-one years old. He first started digging underground by working on the Boston subway system. He soon found that working for wages did not offer the freedom he was looking for in this country. From Boston he moved to California in 1904 to start a fruit orchard for grafting citrus fruit trees. Finding the climate unlike the cool Mediterranean Coast that he was used to and finding the soil unfertile and encrusted with hardpan, he decided to make his home and orchard underground. For forty years he dug underground making a home approximately seven acres in size. Since he was his own architect and designer he did not make a plan but planned as he dug. His main tools were hand tools, a pick, a shovel and wheelbarrow; a horse and a small scraper were used to move large rocks. He dug over ninety rooms, passages and courts each with an open hole to the surface for light and water for a fruit tree immediately below. He dug most of the rooms ten feet below the surface, a small lower level twenty-two feet below and another few rooms thirty-five feet below the surface. His big dream was a restaurant underground. He dug a seven hundred foot long automobile tunnel to service the restaurant, and had started a five thousand square foot room, but he died in 1946 before he finished his project.

His main love was grafting fruit trees which was the main reason for digging underground. On one tree he grafted seven different citrus fruits: navel oranges, sour and sweet lemons, grapefruit, tangerines and Sicilian lemons. He believed that fruit would grow better below ground and that controlled sunlight would permit faster and healthier growth. The temperature outside could often be 120° whereas underground it would remain at 70° throughout the year. Loam was brought for the trees to replace the hardpan. Each tree is grown in a circular planter and has a hole above to catch the sun and rain.

"All that I have done is nothing, for it required very little money—perhaps $300."

1. Entrance
2. Entrance Hall
3. Planter
4. Well
5. Living Room
6. Kitchen
7. Church
8. Chapel
9. Automobile Tunnel
10. Pedestrian Tunnel
11. Winery
12. Light Well
13. Stairs
14. Walkway
15. Patio

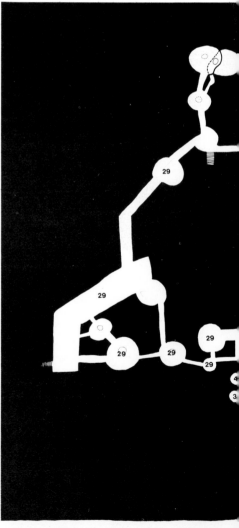

16. Sump Pit
17. Hothouse
18. Indoor Patio
19. Bedroom
20. Bedroom Court
21. Bathroom
22. Reading Room
23. Stairs to Lower Level
24. Tunnel Under
25. Glass Bottom Aquarium
26. Nursery
27. Restaurant (incomplete)
28. Kitchen
29. Unopened

30 20 10 0

His original living areas consisted of two spaces, a living room with seats carved in the wall and a kitchen. Later he dug a larger living area with a living room, dining room, kitchen and two bedrooms. In the living room he built a fireplace for heat in the winter. In his bedroom was a hole above his bed and the early morning light would awaken him. Whenever he needed a space to put an object he would simply carve a niche. Outside his kitchen is a pond with a bridge over it where he kept fish.

In addition to plants Forestiere loved fish. So he built a tropical aquarium. The bottom of the aquarium is glass and in the room underneath he could sit and study the habits of his fish.

"I have been doing this for fun. Money? What do I want with money? If I had $1,000,000 I couldn't spend it. Neither could you. Nobody could. I am broke but this cavern and all the work it represents is worth more than $1,000,000 to me."

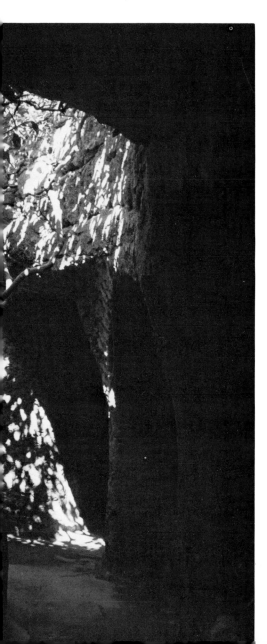

# EMANUELE DAMONTE
Pope Valley, California

Hubcaps, birdhouses, signs and cast-offs that people had no use for, Emanuele (Litto) used to make his place. He is a retired cement finisher, and when he worked in San Francisco he would put designs on the concrete. He came from Italy when he was nineteen. There he helped his father do marble and mosaic floors. He built this place for his home to say "This is Litto."

"I got here in this valley in 1942. You know when I got this place there was nothing here, all clay. So I started to bring some rock from the cliff over there for the driveway. But people when they come they used to turn around here and kept knocking the rocks all over, so I says, by golly I'm gonna fix those people and I built this."

"So everything you see I build. The birdhouse I start by building just for fun for the birds one or two, now I don't know there are two hundred of them. And I have about four hundred hubcaps. And people bring signs, they say, Hey Litto, another sign. I find a place for it, you see all those signs they bring me. The church club, the mother club, the school club, they do rummage sales, everything left, they say let's bring it to Litto."

"Lot of junk this — that's all, lot of junk."

# WILLIE OWSLEY
Hindman, Kentucky

He builds chairs, music boxes, baskets, sawmills and houses. He is a farmer. He designs houses on the back of each month of the Chesapeake and Ohio Railroad calendars so as not to waste paper. He collects the memories of his life and puts them into his home. A calendar of his life.

Willie Owsley was born in 1898 and has spent his life farming and making objects. His father taught him the crafts he practices. Now he is concerned that the younger generation will not have a craft or know how to do the things that have been done for years. He believes that people should know how to do for themselves.

"In them walls there's bottles, sometimes marbles, one fool thing and another, I don't know what all. All things from rocks, horseshoes and oxen shoes. Anything from a set of dice and up. I've got rock in the house from all fifty states. That big round rock in there is a mill stone from my grandmother, good lord that thing's over a hundred years old. I ate mill from corn bread when I was a kid."

"I built the house all by myself. If I had to do it over again I build the whole thing out of cobblestone. I've got some cobblestone in the walls from the state of Maine. I've got rock from all fifty states in the walls."

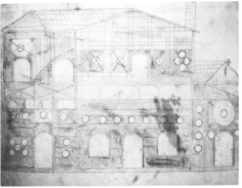

"I just had the eighth grade of schooling way back, and I can make blueprints that make your head hurt, they're so complicated. I can show you a lot of mansions I drew, but I never made a picture of this house, I just went ahead and built it."

"If somebody don't teach somebody how to make things, the younger generation will have to fall onto something else. By Ned there's nobody hardly knows what a scrub broom is these days, but I can make one out of hickory. Young people need to know how to do for themselves."

"No sir, I was a poor man when I first started out and I'm just as poor now today. I raised ten head of youngens. When you raised ten of them you're going to be out lot of money. Back then I'd farm a lot of four to five hundred acres of land you know. Raised my own meat and stuff and get your own milk, I had four or five head of cows and thirty to forty head of hogs, that meant something then. Now today you bought a little piece of meat you get about three or four bites and it'll cost you a dollar."

"Back in them days I raised all my food. There were a few things you had to buy—flour to make biscuits out of it. Some things you know, your sugar you had to buy, but gee whiz, you could buy a ten pound of sugar then for 39 or 40 cents, trade hen eggs for it. We had a big bunch of chickens, more than we could use and take them to these restaurants and sell the eggs, exchange it for the stuff we didn't have. You know that means a lot."

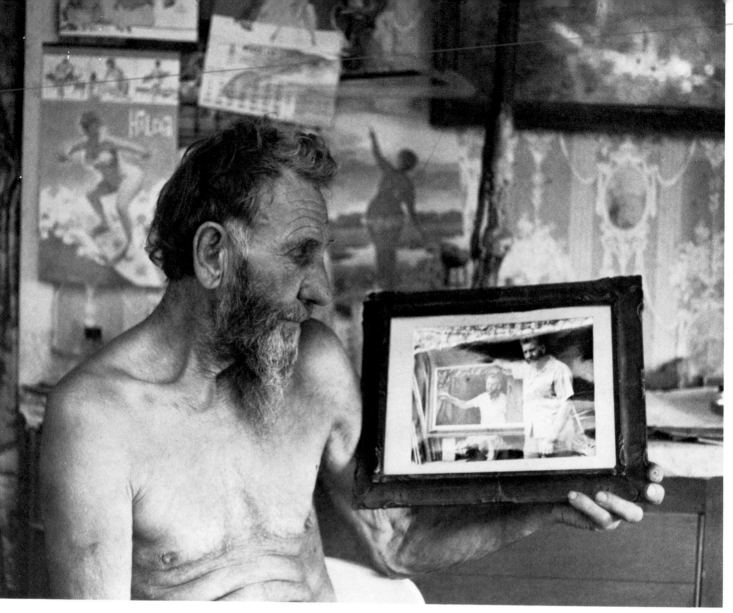

# ART BEAL
West Cambria Pines, California

Art Beal, Dr. Tinkerpaws and Captain Nitwitt are all the same
man. Beal, because it was his father's name; Tinkerpaws, because
he tinkers with his hands; and Nitwitt because he lives on Nitwitt
Ridge. He was born seventy-seven years ago in San Francisco. He

has been building for forty-five years in Cambria Pines. During that time he did not buy any materials, except for a little "baking powder and flour"—cement and sand. He has grown his food, even sharing it with his neighbors. Now some of his neighbors think his home is an eyesore and should be bulldozed. His home is built up the side of a rock cliff 250 feet high. There are nine levels connected by stairs and two to three rooms on each level. His materials were cast-offs that he found along his travels: abalone shells, beer cans, tires, car wheels, pots and pans.

"It was in 1928 when it all began. Nobody was here then. This hill was hidden far back in the woods. So, I created my first one-room shack. But that wasn't enough. I put up another and another and another. I can't stop now."

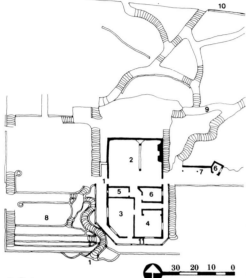

1. Entrance
2. Living Room
3. Kitchen
4. Bedroom
5. Storage
6. Bathroom
7. Workshop
8. Terrace Garden
9. Steps
10. Storage Shed
11. Porch

"Well you see the majority of people today, they're born in these man-made mountains of concrete, steel, asbestos and asphalt. They get out and maybe they go to school and get down there and go to work. At the end of the week, here little doggie, here is your bone, now make it last until next week. Well, they're like a canary in a cage. You turn them out here in freedom. What do they know. They starve to death in the midst of plenty."

"You can't rush things. You got to have a solid footing, but don't rush things. And when it's solid it's hard to break. It takes time to build a footing. This place took a couple of nights, a few days, and then a few more days and a couple of nights."

"You got to do. You got to show. You got to do. And when they see: Well, look what he has done."

"Beauty is a fairer shore,
Beauty shines for evermore."

Railings for steps and walls are made from water pipes which also are used for irrigating his gardens. He grows what he eats: tomatoes, potatoes, beans, apricots and citrus fruits.

"Time means nothing to me. The tide comes and goes. Time never returns. I'll worry about time when I'm in the marble orchard."

"Everything is junk I picked up along life's travels."

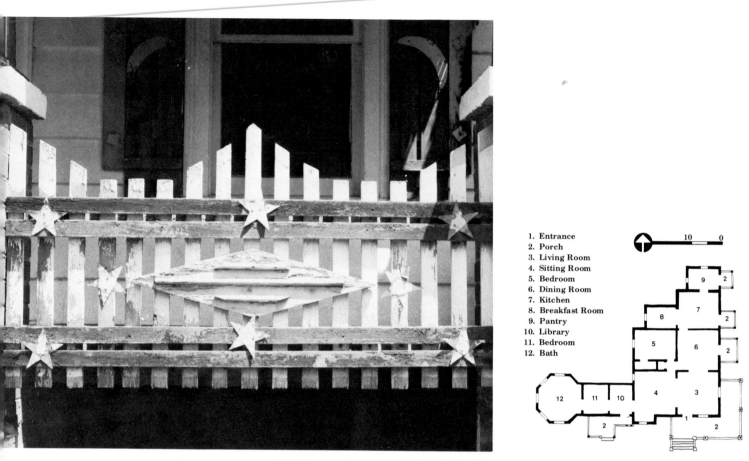

1. Entrance
2. Porch
3. Living Room
4. Sitting Room
5. Bedroom
6. Dining Room
7. Kitchen
8. Breakfast Room
9. Pantry
10. Library
11. Bedroom
12. Bath

# WILLIAM J. PRESTON, SR.
Shawsville, Virginia

It has sat on the hill above the road for over thirty years. It has acted as a guidepost for many motorists. Some thought it was a dream or a fairy tale. Some thought a nightmare or a joke. Some thought it silly and foolish to spend so much time building such a place. But some stopped and admired.

William Preston was born in Virginia in 1901 and lived most of his life around Shawsville. He has had many trades during his life, while slowly over the years he built his dream house known as the "Gingerbread House."

"When I first bought the land I didn't do anything but clean the land. It was in brush and then I just started building before it got cold. And at first I built four rooms. And then I had to go to work, and then I came back and built a little more until now there are ten rooms, a hall, two closets, five porches and all of them different."

"Well, I needed a home and I decided I was going to build one. You couldn't find a piece of land hardly to save your neck around here. And then when I started to build you couldn't get no one to build at that time. So I just decided I'd make a plan in my mind and build it myself and that's what I did."

"Well I wanted the balls on top and I didn't have time to cut them and you couldn't get no one to do it, so I got these toilet ball floats and they will last forever. And each one is different, and that was my idea. I wanted on one the moon, with the big star and I just decided for each what I wanted on them and did it."

"I started building in 1940-41 and then I added some more as I went along. I didn't do it all at once because I was working."

"I have been in the ministry for forty-six years, and I got trades I have learnt as I was growing up. I can do any kind of mill work, I do carpentry work, I do cabinet work. I'm a textile printer by trade and I'm a veterinarian."

"My main idea is not to be like somebody else. Too many people today wants to be like the other bird. They want to be like somebody else, not themselves. I think God gave us all a mind to do things for ourselves, to think for ourselves."

# ROMANO GABRIEL
Eureka, California

We asked at the garage if they had heard of the man who built a wooden garden. It had to be in this area, not more than a couple of blocks away. But the people at the garage had never heard of it; they thought the man next door, who had lived there all his life, might know. He was sure that was Romano's place but thought it had been torn down. The town had considered it an eyesore and firetrap, and had been trying to get it removed. If it still was around, then it would be up the hill and he pointed out the area where it might be. We walked up the hill and down the streets not knowing exactly what we were looking for but knowing we would know it if we saw it. Then there it was only two blocks from the garage. The sun made one of its rare appearances in Eureka and the colors were bright against the blue sky. A wooden garden.

Romano Gabriel came to this country in 1913 from Italy. There he worked with his father who was a furniture maker. Here he served in World War I and then moved to Eureka. He has been a carpenter, having built nine houses, has worked in the lumber yards and as a gardener. He built his present home and then slowly built his garden, working on it for the last thirty years. The first objects he built were trees and flowers, some of which move in the wind. Later he added animals, some that turn like carousels. Finally he made faces of people he heard of or knew.

Slowly his home has disappeared behind the wooden flowers, faces
and animals. Most of the pieces were made from the ends and sides
of wooden orange crates. At first he used a hand saw to cut the
pieces, later he built a small power circular saw. Each year until
recently the garden has been newly painted.

"My idea was just to make these things, I just wanted to make something different. I just made up pictures out of wood. I don't buy any materials, I take all the boxes and lumber down in the store, they are all ends of fruit boxes."

His sources of inspiration have been memories of people and places he has seen and the National Geographic magazine which he receives each month.

"I make one piece at a time but
I no make things now for four
or five years. No more room, no
more boxes. Now all the boxes
they come in paper, no wood."

"I used to be a gardener here in Eureka. Eureka is bad place for flowers, the salty air and no sun. So I just make this garden."

# FATHER MATTHIAS WERNERUS

Dickeyville, Wisconsin

Father Wernerus was born in Germany in 1873 and came to this country in 1904. He was appointed pastor of Holy Ghost Parish in Dickeyville in 1916. Dickeyville was a small farm community of around 100 people.

His first efforts in helping the community were to raise funds for a new school and other improvements. In 1926 he started building the Grotto and continued to build until he died in 1931. In addition to the Grotto, he built walls, cemetery shrines, a monument to Christopher Columbus, flowerpots, fences, birdhouses and flags. His materials were concrete and stones, marbles, shells, molten glass, uncut gems, petrified wood, and most important, what people would bring him. They gave broken plates, glass and cherished objects, all which he incorporated in the building. He also went around the country looking for special rocks and wrote letters throughout the country asking for stones. Most of the glass he melted in a glass furnace and formed in the basement of the rectory.

Mary Wernerus, his housekeeper and cousin, was a co-worker doing most of the layout and planning of the work. During the winter the rectory looked like a rock shop as they would lay out the sections of the work for construction the next spring. He built by shaping steel and covering it with fence wire; then covering the frame with concrete and finally setting the material in the wet concrete. In this way he made small sections and pieced them together. People would help him raise the larger sections, but perhaps most importantly helped by providing materials and objects that shaped and designed the work as it progressed making the total a project of the people. Some of his friends who worked with him talk about his work.

The largest element, the Grotto, stands between the church and the rectory. He finished it in 1930 and many people donated hours of labor, materials and money to finish it.

"It was a hobby to him when he first came to Dickeyville, he kept chickens, rabbits and vineyards, and did a top notch job with them. But he got bored with that and needed something else."

The patriotic shrine is to the people of this country, not only in the history of the country and leaders but in the stories of lives of the people. The work depended to a large extent on what people would bring to become part of the work.

"He didn't fool any time away, it was all work to him, when people stopped, he'd talk a little, but not much."

"He learned as he went. Started out knowing what he wanted to build and then experimented and got it done by trial and error. On one occasion he cemented himself into one unit, and had to chip his way out."

He started the main units by laying footings in a horseshoe shape. These footings four feet deep were built up of concrete and large boulders. His tools consisted of a trowel, shovel and cement mixer.

"One time a friend asked him if he had any idea when he started that it would come to such an extensive thing. He said, 'No, it just came to me as I worked.'"

# ELIS STENMAN
Pigeon Cove, Massachusetts

Elis Stenman, a machine designer, thought that something should be done with old newspapers that usually are thrown away. He experimented with rolling newspapers in a way that would not destroy the print. Then he and his wife started to build a house. They began in 1922 and continued for the next twenty years until he died in 1942. The walls and roof of the house are made from 215 sheets of newspaper pasted and folded into different designs.

After building the house they discovered new uses for the papers. By rolling the papers into very tight, small cylinders they were able to use them structurally like Lincoln Logs. With this idea they made chairs and benches, tables, lamps, a piano, a clock and even a fireplace.

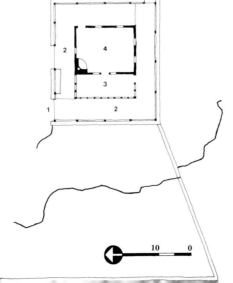

1. Entrance
2. Covered Porch
3. Enclosed Porch
4. Living Room

10   0

Approximately 100,000 copies of newspapers have been used in building the house and furniture. The rolls can be unwound and the print inside will be preserved, since neither glue nor varnish was used in making the paper rolls.

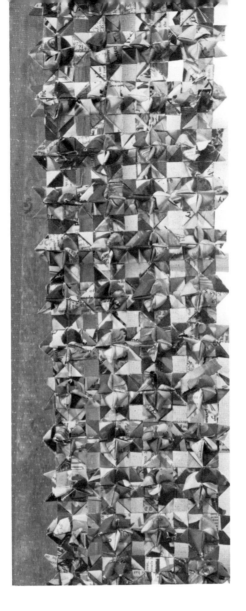

Curtains were made by folding and weaving colored newspapers.
The clock was made from newspaper of major cities in the country.

# CABOT YERXA
Desert Hot Springs, California

He started building when he was sixty and continued until he died at eighty-three in 1965. Cabot Yerxa was born in the Dakota Territory and lived his early life in Minnesota. When the Gold Rush in the Yukon came he decided to go. But not for gold. Instead, he set up a tent and sold tobacco. In 1908 he and his burro homesteaded 160 acres at Desert Hot Springs. While digging for water one day he discovered the hot springs.

He joined the army in World War I and did not return until 1937. Shortly after his return he started building the pueblo. He used lumber found on the desert left over from the All American Canal, salvaged nails and used the native soil adobe. When he had finished the pueblo contained thirty-five rooms on several levels.

Towards the end of his life he started a second home up the hill from the first. He died before he had finished. The buildings are still there being looked after and added to by his friend, Colbert Eyrand.

One of the reasons for building the pueblo was to make Indians who visited him feel at home. The structure was built in the character of Hopi architecture. In addition to a home for himself the pueblo contains a museum of Indian history.

30 20 10 0

1. Entrance
2. Courtyard
3. Storage
4. Workshops
5. Bathroom
6. Store
7. Hall
8. Art Gallery
9. Office
10. Kitchen
11. Dining Room
12. Living Room
13. Bedroom
14. Reservoir
15. Guest House (incomplete)
16. Barn

127

The pueblo grew over a period of twenty-three years and now contains thirty-five rooms in four stories. Sketches were made but no plans and the building grew as materials became available.

# HERMAN RUSCH
Cochrane, Wisconsin

Off the main highway and down a dirt road with the dust billowing
behind. Around a curve past a fence like no other to see a man like
no other. Herman Rusch, born in 1886, lover of nature, a farmer
and a builder who wanted to leave something behind—a story of
his thoughts.

1. Entrance
2. Museum
3. Arched Fence
4. Arches
5. Flower Planter
6. Stone Birdhouse
7. Fountain
8. Hindu Temple
9. Watch Tower
10. Round Spiral
11. Square Tower
12. Indian on Horse
13. Concrete Cactus
14. Vase
15. Boat
16. Stone Post
17. Concrete Mountain
18. Concrete Snake
19. Stone House
20. Dinosaur

40 30 20 10 0

"Like it says mister, a fellow should leave a few tracks and not just cancelled welfare checks."

"We farmed forty years, and then I don't know, and then we retired four years, and then I got this notion about this museum. You know, pick up some oddities and things like that. My idea was that I had no irons in the fire of my own so we rented this place, it was the former dance pavilion, they called it Prairie Moon. And there was nothing out here just a big parking place that looked empty. So I builds this first rock pile. Well then I thought it still looks kinda lonely and then I builds a little bigger one that had four tiers coming down. After that I got some ideas, you know, and then I had about two or three projects ahead while I was building. I had no idea that this would look like anything like this you know when I started."

"The fence, I can tell you how I made it. I had two posts here and one arch, these two posts and then one arch. So I said to my brother-in-law, by golly if I put another post there I could make another arch. He says that's good enough. Well, I couldn't understand on a place like this when you can make it better than good enough, then you better be at it. Don't you think so? So then a little later I put this arch over here. Well, that's all you could do. But then when I had these three posts and those two arches, by golly, I says, wouldn't that make a nice fence along the road. But I thought that was too much work. Well, then one fall, you know late in the fall, it was the last week in October, by golly, doing nothing again I goes at it. I started there in the last week in October. It have to be fairly warm, that's mostly hard work, you can't work there when it's zero and the wind blowing you know. That fall and November was warm. I worked three weeks in November and by golly I put in fifteen posts and that gate post and they weren't all pointed out you know and no arches in, but I put in fifteen posts. Next year you know I took care of the whole business and cut the grass. The lawn wasn't as big as it is now. Few people come, not so many yet, and the second year when I got started I had that fence done in one year and those points I made down cellar."

"At my next birthday I'll be eighty-eight you know, that rock seems to be getting heavier. I just wish I were fifty years younger, you know, the longer I live the better life gets."

The fence of arches is 260 feet long, is made of cast-in-place, built-up and precast concrete. It was all assembled in one summer, and the concrete is dyed, so that the color will last longer. As the concrete sets he adds pebbles, mirrors and pieces of broken pottery.

# CHARLES CASKIN
Yuma, Arizona

Driftwood Charlie was not there. He had gone into town for supplies and would be back soon. We waited, and played a game of dominoes with his friend in the shade of his trailer. It was hot. Finally the noise of the Winnebago was heard and soon Driftwood Charlie appeared.

He talked about everything from art to politics and particularly concentrated on the problems of this country.

Charles Caskin was born in Arkansas. He has been in the navy most of his life and been all over the world. In 1947 when he was retiring, doctors told him that he had a short time to live. They suggested that he move to the hottest and dryest climate he could find. He moved to Death Valley where he stayed for fifteen years and then in 1960 moved on to Yuma, Arizona. Here he has been making what he calls "Charley's World of Lost Art." He carves from soft stone and concrete images that he remembered on his trips, some pertaining to the Bible.

"It's beginning to be inhuman out in this country. If you go along and look at the trash they leave when they go in the spring a great many people have no respect for others."

140

The sculptures are placed in an area over an acre in size. Charles Caskin lives in a trailer in the middle of his creations.

"I used to do a lot of engraving years ago. I'm an old retired navy man. Those days I could make anything I wanted to, from this to that. Today most of the people in this country don't think for themselves."

His themes are from the Bible and ancient history, but some are more current, such as an astronaut hitching a ride.

"I carve these all out when they're wet. I rough out the thing but the details are carved out while they're still wet. My best weapon is a beer can opener."

"If you have a creative mind and can visualize any face or feature of anything you got it made. That is two secrets I found you got to have. If you have not that ability you might as well throw your trowel away and the cement over the wall and hide and see how it runs."

Some sculptures appear to grow from the native stone; the concrete objects are made by forming a wire frame, pouring concrete over and carving the details while still wet.

# HENRY DORSEY
Brownsboro, Kentucky

After the man had filled the bus with gasoline, we asked if he knew of an unusual place around here. Without looking at us he said we must mean "the attraction—that's what we call it around here." He pointed across the road to a street and said we couldn't miss it.

Henry Dorsey's place is not a place to miss. The house built close to the road is difficult to see at first. Between it and the road seems to be everything. Tires, toys, rims, display cases, hubcaps, refrigerators, clocks, bottles, radiators, toys, shells, bicycles, lamps, pictures, toys, photographs, plastic pieces, cans, plastic animals, tires, toys, wagon wheels, lights, dish pans, windows, hobby horses and more tires and toys. Everything. Some turn around, some move up and down, some have lights that flash on and off and some cause chain reactions of movement when a switch is turned.

Henry Dorsey has been building for many years. Some call him a "tinker" or "toyman" but neither of these tell the complete story. He is more—a builder. When Henry Dorsey became deaf he started building. He is a self-taught electrician, stone mason, carpenter and builder. People would bring him toys, animals and cast-offs and he would build with them. He was not creating a piece of art—just building.

151

"I've got to keep myself busy all the time or else I would lose my mind."

Most of his work is between the house and road, but in addition he has worked on the house and built sculptures in the yard from cans and tires.

# ALFRED RICCIUTI
Buffalo, New York

Alfred Ricciuti is a poet, a builder, a collector and a bus driver. He has written poems about politics and the problems he has had with the city about his home. He is a stone mason, building his home with stone he has salvaged. He collects cameras, paintings and bells. He has been working slowly on building his home for the last ten years. The neighbors and city think his place is an eyesore and have constantly tried to have it torn down. They think he is not building fast enough. But any building under construction looks unfinished and undone. So far with the help of friends, he is still there.

"Individuals will all build differently if they build for their individuality. And this would make for a tremendous variety, and make for pride. Any man building for himself will build better if he understands the techniques of building. These craftsmen who put up buildings rapidly have to do it because they have to get out so much work. They have to cut corners. They have to use materials that you wouldn't use if you were building for yourself. The buildings they put up are not designed to last. But if a man was building for his own family he would build a house that would stand not only for his lifetime but for his children's and grandchildren's. This is the mark of a society or culture that is mature and thinks it is going to continue to exist. But we in America have had sort of pioneer tradition, build a shack, take over some land and till it for awhile, perhaps run it dry and then move on."

"I started working on the house when I was not only broke but in debt. Then I was presented with a very difficult task, I had very little time too, as I was driving a bus. But I had stone. It was left over from a landscape business that hadn't been too saleable. I had an accumulation of a great many kinds of stone that I had been saving for possible use in this house. So I utilized what I had at hand. It was the cheapest way, in fact builders always utilize, when they're building efficiently, what's around."

1. Entrance
2. Hall
3. Bedroom
4. Bathroom
5. Living Room
6. Future Terrace

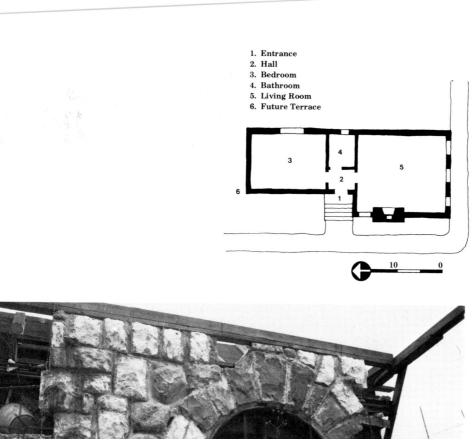

"I've drawn some of the plans up, but most of it is in my head. This way I can revise the plans without great changes on paper."

"Every man needs a fortress of the human spirit. This is the expression of one man's unshackled mind."

# GEORGE PLUMB
Duncan, British Columbia

George Plumb, a carpenter, started with 5,000 bottles in 1963 and has been building ever since, using over 180,000 bottles. He thought that most carpenters ended their life's work with only a bent back and wanted to leave something more substantial.

Bottles have come from neighbors, from visitors and from industries. He has used every kind there is. Jam bottles, pop bottles, milk, coke, beer bottles, liquor bottles and medicine bottles of every shade and size make up his home.

In addition to his home he has built many other buildings of bottles. Around the buildings stand animals he has carved out of concrete. He is still working on the buildings and now carves small animals from stone.

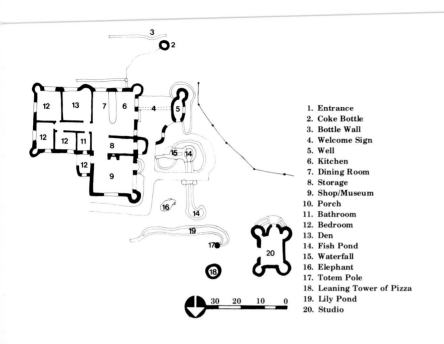

1. Entrance
2. Coke Bottle
3. Bottle Wall
4. Welcome Sign
5. Well
6. Kitchen
7. Dining Room
8. Storage
9. Shop/Museum
10. Porch
11. Bathroom
12. Bedroom
13. Den
14. Fish Pond
15. Waterfall
16. Elephant
17. Totem Pole
18. Leaning Tower of Pizza
19. Lily Pond
20. Studio

30  20  10  0

"I used to be a carpenter. I did the odd fireplace in my time, stone walls and stuff like that too. Whenever somebody wanted something built, I always figured I could build it. I never turned down anything yet."

# FRED BURNS
Belfast, Maine

Fred Burns was born in Maine eighty-seven years ago. He has been a hunter, trapper and guide and served in World War I. He has lived for the last thirty-six years on the Harbor below the chicken factory which provides him with a steady supply of chickens for Fred and his dogs. He has ten dogs. He built his home from materials he found on the beach and painted it with left-over paint.

"Just a little bit different from anyone else."

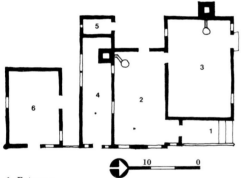

1. Entrance
2. Kitchen/Living
3. Bedroom
4. Storage
5. Bathroom
6. Shed

10    0

"I was a boy. My mother died, my father died. You remember those days when it was so hard you couldn't get no work or nothing. An' I said, by golly, I'm going to do something. I tramped along the road, met some good people, you know, farmers, and I picked some potatoes. Of course, I could pick a lot of potatoes in those days. I beat them all. Then I was drafted in the First World War."

"I only had $12.50 when I come here. And I said, by golly, I'm going to try and live. And I catch some fish here. A man starving to death will eat anything, won't he? Then the poultry plant come in and build a big factory here. I went up, and I worked there a while, till I got so I couldn't. And today, I got a place to live anyhow."

"It's just something different. All I done was pick up driftwood off the beach and nails. I bend old rusty nails and I built it a little at a time, and left over paint I got from five gallon cans."

"I live alone and I love everybody, that's the only way to be."

"We could not believe we had built it because it seemed to us incredibly big, and quite incredibly beautiful. The setting sun brought out a rosy-saffron color in the mud bricks, and laid across them long violet shadows, with highlights of yellow. Since it was made of the earth on which it stood, it had serenity about it, as if it had been there always. 'We never built it,' we whispered. 'No one built it, it materialized out of a dream.'

# MAUDE MEAGHER
# CAROLYN SMILEY
Los Gatos, California

Maude Meagher and Carolyn Smiley ran a publishing house in Boston producing a magazine entitled "World Youth Today." Their magazine was circulated throughout the world. During World War II it became impossible to circulate their magazine. So in 1940 they left Boston and bought land in California to realize their dream— to build a home and printing office. They knew nothing about building but were determined that they could do what others have done. They did not have builders' or architects' plans—just ideas.

They chose mud as their main material making adobe blocks by hand. They worked for fifteen years building a structure over 15,000 square feet.

"We knew nothing whatever about building. We had never done any rough work. One of us was a writer, the other a lecturer and educator with book binding and amateur movies as her hobbies. But we both had college degrees, and we assumed that since primitive people can build their own adobe houses, we could too, if we put our minds to it, solving each problem as it came up."

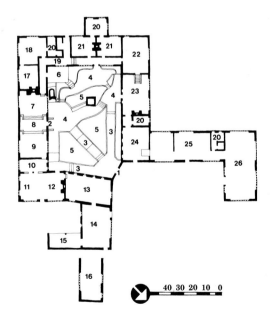

1. Gate
2. Entrance
3. Walk/Stairs
4. Terrace
5. Garden
6. Porch
7. Living Room
8. Entrance Hall
9. Dining Room
10. Tea Room
11. Kitchen
12. Breakfast Room
13. Storage Room
14. Garage
15. Wood Shed
16. Storage Shed
17. Living/Study
18. Caroline Smiley Bedroom
19. Hall
20. Bathroom
21. Guest Bedroom
22. Maude Meagher Bedroom
23. Living/Study
24. Library/Office
25. Workroom
26. Printing Room

40 30 20 10 0

"We were guided in our digging by lines of string which we had laid out one January day. That was a wonderful day of plans and dreams. While looking for our site we had made various sketches on the backs of old envelopes, and even larger plans, on sheets of typing paper, scaled a quarter inch to the foot. None of these plans suited the ground we finally decided upon as ours, for the lines of a house, we feel, should be adapted to the contour of the earth it stands on. This is particularly true of a mud-brick house, for one might say that it grows out of the earth as a tree grows, and remains even more visibly a part of that earth."

"So we discarded all our plans, and let the contours of our little plot of two acres decide the shape of the house that was to grow from it. We broke up some orange crates and made stakes of them to indicate the corners of the rooms that were to be. Then, zigzagging up the gentle slope and around again to make an enclosed patio, we stretched our lines of string to indicate the ground plan."

"The low, earth-colored walls of the house looked as if they had grown out of the soil, as indeed they had. It was hard for us, even then, to remember we had placed them there. Little friendly lizards ran over their yellow-brown surfaces, or basked in the sun contentedly. The house already belonged to itself, to the land, to the lizards, to the trees—not at all to us."

179

"We read our booklets, but the key words in them were technical and incomprehensible to us. They were written by people who knew what they were talking about because they had already put on roofs. We hadn't, so we didn't know what their words meant. Now we can read their pamphlets intelligently because we have put up a roof ourselves and know what they mean by their words."

"Ignorant people can't afford to take chances, and we didn't. We were very, very careful, testing everything and bolting everything that could be bolted."

"We had learned by now that if you start making a hand-made house you must go on with it in the same way, since you are not likely to find stock sizes to fit the odd angles that result, and which, we think, give hand-work a spontaneous and legitimately picturesque quality. Se we decided to buy the glass and cut the pieces, one by one, to fit the spaces for which they were intended."

"It seems that a law had been passed making it mandatory to use nonshatterable glass in automobile windows and windshields. Consequently the auto wrecking yards were stacked with many hundreds of discarded windshields made of good heavy plate glass. We bought several hundred of these for a very low price and we bought some glass cutters at the dime store. We asked the dealer to show us how to use the cutters."

"It was a great temptation to skimp the time required for a thorough drying out of the cement in the firebox. Two full weeks are necessary, at least when the partition wall happens to be adobe, for if a fire is lighted too soon the concrete may crack. At last the time for testing whether or not the completed fireplace would draw came, and with trembling fingers we laid in paper and wood."

"A beautiful great fan of flame arose and not a shred of smoke. We sat on the cold concrete floor in front of it and hugged our knees. Then we went out into the patio to see if the smoke were actually coming out of the chimney. It was, and all the air outside was adrift with the sweet spicy scent of burning prunewood. Casa Tierra had become a home."

# HARRY D. ANDREWS
Loveland, Ohio

In 1929 Harry D. Andrews started building a dream for his Sunday School kids on the land where the castle stands. He would camp out in tents with his Sunday School class. After the third year the tents became worn and so he started building a stone tent. He made two rooms, now the bottoms of the tower. He did not build much during the Depression and after he started again, he averaged only an hour a week. In 1955 he retired from a Cincinnati publishing firm as a writer and proofreader and worked full time on the castle. For almost twenty years he has been building the castle, still working on it now to build a round tower addition. He is now 84 years old.

He calls it "Chateau Laroche," made of rock he gathered from the river below. The rock is backed up by concrete blocks made by pouring concrete in milk cartons. People have for years brought him empty milk cartons. Empty oil cans provide reinforcing for the roofs of the main rooms. The castle is 96′ by 65′ with one tower 36′ high.

Many young people, who belong to the Knights of the Golden Trail, Inc., an organization Andrews started, helped work on the castle. They have carved their initials in the stone.

In addition to the building on the castle he has built terraces and cold frames to grow some of his food.

"I have been building for forty-four years and still working on it. It's slow work for one man."

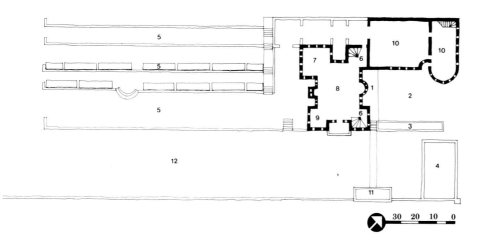

1. Entrance
2. Courtyard
3. Planting
4. Garage
5. Terrace Garden
6. Stairs
7. Kitchen
8. Main Room
9. Study
10. Workroom (incomplete)
11. Storage Room (incomplete)
12. Garden

30  20  10  0

# S.P. DINSMOOR
Lucas, Kansas

It was 112° and they said it might get hot in the afternoon. The road to Lucas was through desolate scorched land, no one in sight. And then finally Lucas—population 620. And then the search for the Garden of Eden, down all streets, looking both ways—was it a joke? Did it exist? And then finally through the sweat, like a mirage standing on the corner. It was truly a Garden of Eden.

Samuel Perry Dinsmoor was born in Ohio in 1843, fought in the Civil War and taught school in Illinois in 1866. He moved to Nebraska and then finally to Kansas where he farmed in 1905. He retired from farming and moved into the town of Lucas.

He started this part of his life by building his "cabin home," a house with eleven rooms, bath, electricity and made from limestone blocks and concrete. It was here that he first experimented with concrete using bottles for form work. He started making the 150 pieces of sculpture by first building his idea of the "Garden of Eden."

He thought in this world there should be a physical representation of the Bible's story of the Garden of Eden. In addition, he built sculptural comments depicting modern civilization and its problems, concrete American flags, political commentaries, his mausoleum and cages for badgers, coyotes and birds. The sculptures are made of concrete molded wet over chicken wire, sometimes forty feet high. Each sculpture has lights above or as features of the work, so that they could be lighted at night. He had built his generating plant for electricity.

In 1924 when eighty-one years old, he married a woman twenty years old and a daughter was born in 1926. S.P. Dinsmoor died in 1932, at the age of eighty-nine. He lies in the mausoleum in a specially built coffin of concrete he designed and built.

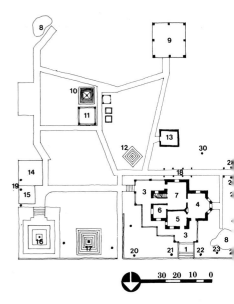

1. Entrance to House
2. Entrance to Garden of Eden
3. Porch
4. Living Area
5. Den
6. Bedroom
7. Study
8. Pool
9. Dining Hall
10. Badger & Pigeon Roost
11. Coyote & Eagle Roost
12. Strawberry Bed
13. Washhouse
14. Car Shed
15. Coal House
16. Mausoleum
17. Goddess of Liberty Tree
18. Snake Grape Arbor
19. Crucifixion of Labor
20. Dog Tree
21. Indian Tree
22. Soldier Tree
23. Trust Tree
24. Cain & Wife Tree
25. Burial Tree
26. Cain & Abel Tree
27. Adam Tree
28. Eve Tree
29. Stork Tree
30. Devil Tree

Mausolium in Garden of Eden

"This is my sign—'GARDEN OF EDEN'—I could hear so many, as they go by, sing out, 'What is this?' so I put this sign up. Now they can read it, stop or go on, just as they please."

196

"There is the Goddess of Liberty with one foot on the trusts and a spear in her hand going through the head of the trusts. The trusts' claws are getting nothing. Down below is a man and woman with a cross-cut saw marked ballot, sawing off the charted rights limb that the trust stands on. That shows how we can get away with the trusts and if we don't get away with them with the ballot, they will be shot away with the bullet, as they were in Russia. They are getting too big. They have got all our sugar."

"Here is the soldier with his gun shooting at the Indian on the next tree. Here is the Indian with his bow and arrow shooting at the dog on the next tree. The dog is after the fox, fox after the bird, bird has its mouth open after a little worm eating a leaf. This shows how one animal is after another down to the leaf. Now this side is modern civilization as I see it. If it is not right I am to blame, but if the Garden of Eden is not right Moses is to blame. He wrote it up and I built it."

"I believe Labor has been crucified between a thousand grafters ever since Labor begun, but I could not put them all up, so I have put up the leaders—Lawyer, Doctor, Preacher and Banker. I do not say they are all grafters, but I do say they are the leaders of all who eat cake by the sweat of the other fellow's face. The Lawyer interprets the law. The Doctor has his knife and saw ready to carve up the bones. The Preacher is saying to this poor fellow crucified, 'Never mind your suffering here on earth, my friend, never mind your suffering here, secure home in heaven for A-l-l E-t-e-r-n-i-t-y and you'll be right.' This is the stuff he is giving Labor for his cake. He knows nothing about Eternity and that he does know if he knows anything. What fools we be to sweat to give the other fellow cake. The Banker has the money, takes the interest and breaks up more people than any other class."

# PEOPLE

Part of the travel and research for this book was made possible by the Wheelwright Travelling Fellowship, Harvard Graduate School of Design, Harvard University, 1974. The material first appeared in a travelling exhibition at M.I.T. and Harvard University in 1974 and 1975. Special thanks to Kevin Ruedisueli who worked with me in preparing this material and particularly for drawing the plans. I am also deeply appreciative for the concern and assistance that Marie Kennedy gave during all aspects of this book.

My thanks to Mary Jane Medved, who designed the book, for her extra care and her seeing these places in a way that I couldn't; to Jack D. Howell, Publisher's agent, who helped make it possible to get this project into book form, and to Charlotte Renner, Alfred S. Schenkman and others at Schenkman Publishing Company.

Finally to all the people who have helped in making this book: Lawrence Anderson, Paul Battaglia, Harry L. Burns, Bob Camp, Nanine Clay, Grace Gordon Collins, Selma M. Curtis, Robert Doherty, Nick Elton, Colbert Eyrand, Lorraine Forestiere, Ann Frye, Bill G. Garrett, Tom Gibbs, Dorothy Gibbs, Nancy Goodwin, Mary Lou Gulley, Barbara Haven, Dolores Hayden, Mercedes Hinkson, Mr. and Mrs. James Hubell, Eldon Johnson, Chuck Kennedy, Percy and Gertrude Kennedy, Lance Laver, Dick Levine, Karl Linn, Peter Mackins, Father Malery, Mr. and Mrs. Tripp, Jeannie Winner, Andrew Zalewski.

And to all those people who just took the time to talk with me along the way about building in this country, thank you.

# SOURCES

Many pamphlets, newspaper articles and papers were used in writing this text. Below are listed the items directly used.

Elise Quigley;    *Tulsa World,* Tulsa, Oklahoma
                  —Newspaper article

Baldasare Forestiere;    *The Fresno Bee,* Fresno, California
                         April 30, 1939—Newspaper article

Maude Meagher,
Carolyn Smiley;    "How we Built an Adobe Home House"
                   for *World Youth,* 1950.
                   Maude Meagher,
                   Carolyn Smiley
                   World Youth, Inc.
                   Los Gatos, California

S.P. Dinsmoor;    "The Cabin Home"
                  S.P. Dinsmoor, Lucas, Kansas

# PHOTOGRAPHS

Most of the photographs in this book were taken by the author with 35mm cameras using plus x and kodachrome film. The photographs listed below are the exceptions.

Page number
19 right courtesy of Eldon Johnson
24 left courtesy of Mary Lou Gulley
54 lower left courtesy of Lorraine Forestiere
96, 97, 102, 107 courtesy of Chuck Kennedy
109 courtesy of Dickeyville Grotto
118 courtesy of Selma Curtis
123 right courtesy of Colbert Eyrand
150, 151, 152, 153, 154 courtesy of C.R. Feeney
156 right, 157, 158, 159 courtesy of Andy Zalewski
192, 193, 201, 202 courtesy of Mr. and Mrs. Wayne Naegle

# PRODUCTION CREDITS

Printing, binding, and color separations by Braun-Brumfield, Inc. Type is Century Schoolbook set by Woodland Graphics under the supervision of Harold Scammell. Photographic prints and color duplications by Paul Dupont. The paper is 70# Mead Offset Enamel Dull. Design and production Mary Jane Medved, MJM Studios.